Seven Great Freethinking Philosophers

by
Charles Bradlaugh
&
John C. Wilhelmsson

Revised & Edited
by
John C. Wilhelmsson

ISBN-10: 0990723135

ISBN-13: 978-0990723134

CHAOS TO ORDER
PUBLISHING

San Jose, California

CONTENTS

INTRODUCTION

SEVEN GREAT FREETHINKING PHILOSOPHERS

<u>INTRODUCTION</u>

In an age of conformity brought on by huge cult-like corporations and ubiquitous social media is there still a road less traveled one might choose to follow? How better to confront the conformity of the 21st century than by consulting history's Seven Great Freethinking Philosophers?

We live in a time of stereotypical ignorance: "Christians have narrow minds and oppose diversity," "Muslims value blind faith over reason," and "Women have never made any great contributions to philosophy." Seven Great Freethinking Philosophers crushes these, and many other, myths by detailing how seven great minds fought against conformity in their own ages and left us an inheritance of thought, now almost forgotten, fundamental to such things as human dignity, the scientific method, healthy living, and academic and religious freedom. Based upon "Half-Hours With The Free Thinkers," yet with brand new selections on Augustine, Averroes, and Edith Stein this new version of a classic is a must read for all current, or aspiring, freethinkers.

As an admirer of Charles Bradlaugh's classic works on free thinking I have long wished to bring them, in some form, to a more modern audience. For, although Bradlaugh's works were somewhat overshadowed by the prejudices of his day, one cannot deny the brilliance of the concept or the quality of his research and writing. Thus, I chose to present this current work.

I have sought to take what is best in Bradlaugh and combined it with my own works in order to conduct a review of history's seven great freethinking philosophers. Bradlaugh has generously provided us with selections on Zeno, Epicurus, Descartes, and Spinoza while I have added selections on Augustine, Averroes, and Edith Stein and served as the editor in all.

I am most pleased at this time to present the selection on Averroes. An Islamic Scholar of whom Western Society owns a deeper depth to than it could ever hope to repay.

SEVEN GREAT FREETHINKING PHILOSOPHERS

SEVEN GREAT FREETHINKING PHILOSOPHERS

AUGUSTINE

Augustine was born in 354 A.D. in Thagaste in North Africa. His mother, Monica, was a devout Christian and his father, Patricius, was a Pagan who converted to Christianity on his deathbed. Augustine's ancestors included Berbers, Latins, and Phoenicians although he considered himself to be Punic.

Augustine's family name, Aurelius, suggests that his father's ancestors were freedmen given full Roman citizenship by the Edict of Caracalla in 212 A.D. Augustine's family had been Roman, from a legal standpoint, for at least a century when he was born. It is assumed that his mother Monica, on the basis of her name, was of Berber origin but, as his family was in an upper class of citizens known as honorable men, Augustine's first language was most likely Latin.

At the age of 11, Augustine was sent to school at Madaurus, a small Numidian city about 19 miles south of Thagaste. There he became familiar with Latin literature, as well as pagan beliefs and practices. His first insight into the nature of sin occurred when he and a number of friends stole fruit from a neighborhood garden. He tells this story in his biography "The Confessions." He remembers that he did not steal the fruit because he was hungry, but because it was not permitted.

> *It was foul, and I loved it. I loved my own error—not that for which I erred, but the error itself.*

From this incident he concluded that the human person is naturally inclined to sin.

At the age of 17, through the generosity of his fellow citizen Romanianus, Augustine went to Carthage to continue his education in rhetoric. It was while a student at Carthage that he read Cicero's dialogue "Hortensius" (now lost), which he described as leaving a lasting impression on him and sparking his interest in philosophy. Although raised as a Christian Augustine, much to his mother Monica's despair, eventually left the Church to follow the Manichaean religion. As a youth Augustine lived a hedonistic lifestyle for a time, associating with men who boasted of their sexual exploits. The need to gain acceptance forced boys like Augustine to either seek, or just make up stories about, sexual experiences. And it was during this period that he uttered his famous prayer: *"Grant me chastity and continence, but not yet."*

At about the age of 19, Augustine began an affair with a young woman in Carthage. Although his mother wanted him to marry someone of his class, Augustine remained with this woman for fifteen years and she gave birth to his son Adeodatus. In 385, Augustine ended the relationship in order to prepare to marry a Christian heiress.

Augustine was from the beginning a brilliant student, with an eager intellectual curiosity, yet he never mastered Greek. His first Greek teacher was a harsh man who beat his students, and Augustine rebelled and refused to study (Interestingly enough, the now popular word "Pedagogy" comes from the Greek word "Pedagogue" which describes a person who follows students to school and beats them if they do not study. So the practice of this teacher may not have been that far out of the norm!). By the time Augustine realized that he needed to know Greek, it was too late; and he never became eloquent in it. However, his mastery of Latin was superb as he became both an expert in its eloquent use, and in the making of clever arguments to illustrate his points.

This led him to become a teacher of rhetoric first at Carthage in 375 A.D. and later at Rome in 384 A.D. However, the students in Carthage were unruly and the tradition in Rome was for the students to pay their tuition on the last day of the course. And, despite Augustine's great abilities in the subject, many of his students were not inclined to pay so he began to look for steadier employment.

He found it at Milan and entered into a close relationship with its outstanding bishop Ambrose who, as well as being a great rhetorician and orator in his own right, also served as a civic authority in charge of education. Augustine first began to attend Ambrose's sermons out of a professional curiosity yet soon began to become influenced by his message. This combined with his mother Monica's presence in Milan, and his interest in the Neoplatonic philosophy of Plotinus, caused Augustine to become drawn to the Christian faith of his youth.

The year 386 A.D. was an important one for Augustine's intellectual and spiritual development. First, he converted, or perhaps better "reverted", to Christianity, and then he spent a vacation at Cassiciacum, a rural retreat near Milan, with friends and family. At this time, he completed his first great work of ethics "The Happy Life."

The theme of the discussion in "The Happy Life" is man's desire to be happy. This is an issue of fundamental importance to any person. For, although men do not think of happiness in all of their actions, most everything we do as human beings is related to the search for happiness. Yet Augustine's study of ethics differs from other systems in that it is not a neutral speculation or cold investigation but rather tends toward the welfare of the common person.

In fact, Augustine has been described as the first authentic human person one encounters in history—as the first look into what it really means to be a human being. With his famous quote, *"Grant me chastity and continence, but not yet"*, being a prime example of the dichotomy of the human condition. And by being the first person in history to reveal this authentic human perspective Augustine begins to show his credentials as being one of history's great freethinking philosophers.

However, it is not only in his perspective but also in his method that Augustine shows his originality. For "The Happy Life" is molded upon Cicero's "Hortensius" which was in the form of a Greek dialogue. In classic Greek dialogue the participants were mostly educated males. However, Augustine's dialogue features a woman, a child, and the uneducated with all featured prominently.

Here we are touching upon something quite radical which should not be glossed over. For by including all of these diverse figures in his dialogue Augustine is in fact stating, in the most powerful way possible through his own actions, that philosophy is not just the prerogative of a chosen few but the common good of all irrespective of age, sex, race, or occupation. And it is in this way that Augustine further shows his credentials as a great freethinker and becomes not just a Father of the Church, but the Father of Diversity as well!

And it is not just that a woman and child are present in the dialogue but the fact that their wisdom is featured most prominently in the dialogue that expresses Augustine's true program. For we see in this way that, for Augustine, diversity is not something which should be practiced simply for its own sake but because the greater the diversity within a group of people the greater the chances that their dialogue will present fine insights. And it is in this way that Augustine's argument for diversity is still the finest one.

Augustine dealt with many other problems with a great originality of thought, not the least of which was the age-old problem of evil. This problem is in a sense both a theological and an ethical issue. Stated in a simple form it asks, "If God is all good and created the universe than why is there so much evil within it?" And the lives of many men down through the ages have been effected by their ability to either answer, or not answer, this question.

In the sensual days of his youth Augustine had sought an answer to this question in Manichaeism. Manichaeism featured a theology of a good deity and an evil deity co-existing with equal power, with the good deity being associated with the spiritual and the evil deity being associated with the flesh. The basic solution to the problem of evil being to give each deity its due. Thus, when one was interested in engaging in the things of the spirit the good deity might be honored and when one was interested in engaging in the things of the flesh the evil deity might be honored. However, as time went by Augustine became increasingly intellectually dissatisfied with this solution.

Augustine's ultimately satisfying solution to the problem of evil involves both faith and reason. The faith coming through the prayers of his holy mother Monica and by listening to the eloquent sermons of Ambrose, and the reason coming from one of the last great Neoplatonic philosophers Plotinus.

Plotinus was born in Egypt and lived from 205 to 270 A.D. His system of emanations by "The One" is reminiscent of Plato's Allegory of the Cave in that its symbol for the highest form of truth is the light of the Sun. And just as the light of the Sun shines brightly yet eventually dissipates so do the emanations.

emanations　　The One　　*emanations*

↓　　　The World Soul　　↓

↓　　　The Human Soul　　↓

↓　　　Material Objects　　↓

*******(Realm of Shadows)*******

*******(Darkness)*******

Evil

(As a privation of the Good)

As the emanations flow from "The One" they dissipate to the point of becoming so weak that there exists a realm of shadows. And beyond this point darkness and evil.

Although Plotinus was not a Christian his philosophy formed an almost perfect template for the Christian concept that God is all good and that evil exists only in the darkness that is far away from Him (and thus hidden from His goodness). Both systems also feature a way that man can move either up toward the light or down toward the darkness through his own freewill. With focusing on the spiritual aspects of the universe raising one higher and focusing too much on the material aspects of the universe dragging one down.

Therefore, the problem of evil is seen as something that flows from the gift of freewill which man has been given. For if man uses his freedom to seek what is good, true, and beautiful he can be raised up but if man uses his freedom to seek what is base, false, and common he will be dragged down. Thus it is in the poor use, or perhaps better in the poor understanding, of freedom that mankind drags himself down and brings evil into what was intended to be good.

We have seen that Augustine in his autobiography "Confessions" is the first authentic human being one encounters in history, that in his "The Happy Life" he is a great early champion of diversity, and that in his reading of Plotinus he gives us, through the use of reason, what has become the normative solution to the problem of evil.

Truly given all of this, which does not even begin to exhaust his overall contributions, Augustine has certainly taken his place among history's great freethinking philosophers!

ZENO

Zeno was born at Cittius, a small maritime town in the Island of Cyprus. This place having been originally populated by a colony of Phoenicians, Zeno is sometimes called a Phoenician; but at the period when he flourished, it was chiefly inhabited by Greeks. The date of his birth is uncertain, but must have been about the year 336 B.C. His father was a merchant, and Zeno appears to have been, in the early part of his life, engaged in mercantile pursuits. He received a classical education from his father, whom, we are told, perceived in his son a strong inclination for philosophical studies, and who purchased for Zeno the writings of the Socratic philosophers; which were avidly studied, and which undoubtedly exercised a considerable influence on his future thought. When about thirty years of age, he made a trading voyage from Cittius to Athens, with a very valuable cargo of Phoenician purple dye, but was unfortunately shipwrecked on the coast of Greece, and the whole of his freight destroyed. It is supposed that this severe loss, which must have considerably reduced his means, materially influenced Zeno, and induced him to embrace the tenets of the Cynics, whose leading principle was a contempt of riches. We are told that upon his arrival in Athens, he went into the shop of a bookseller, and took up, by accident, a volume of the "Commentaries of Xenophon." After reading a few pages, Zeno was so delighted with the work, that he asked the bookseller to direct him to where he might meet such men as the author? Crates, the Cynic philosopher, passed by at the time, and the bookseller said, "Follow that man!" He did so, and after listening to several of his discourses, was so pleased with the doctrines of the Cynics, that he became a disciple. He did not long remain attached to the Cynic school—their peculiar manners were too gross for him; and his energetic and inquiring mind was too much cramped by that indifference to all scientific investigation which was one of their leading characteristics. Therefore, he sought instruction elsewhere, and Stilpo, of Megara, became his teacher, from whom he acquired the art of disputation, in which he became very proficient. The Cynics were displeased at his following another school of thought, and we are told that Crates attempted to drag him by force out of the school of Stilpo, on which Zeno said, "You may seize my body, but Stilpo has laid hold of my mind." The Megaric doctrine was, however, insufficient. Zeno was willing to learn all that Stilpo could teach, but having learned all, his restless and insatiable appetite for knowledge required more, and after an attendance of several years upon the lectures of Stilpo, he passed over to the expositors of Plato, Xenocrates, and Polemo. The latter philosopher appears to have penetrated Zeno's design in attending the various schools—i.e., to collect materials from various quarters for a new system of his own; and when he came to the school, Polemo said,

> *I am no stranger, Zeno, to your Phoenician arts; I perceive that your design is to creep slyly into my garden, and steal away my fruit.*

After twenty years of study, having mastered the tenets of the various schools, Zeno determined to become the founder of his own sect. In accordance with this determination, he opened a school in a public portico, called the Painted Porch, from the pictures of Polygnotus, and other eminent painters, with which it was adorned. This portico became famous in Athens, and was called Stoa (the Porch). From this Stoa the school derived its name, the students being called the Stoics.

Zeno was subtle in his reasoning and exceedingly popular. He taught a strict system of morals and exhibited a pleasing picture of moral discipline in his own life. As a man, his character appears deserving of the highest respect. He became exceedingly respected and revered in Athens for the probity and severity of his life and manners, and its consistency with his doctrine. He possessed so large a share of public esteem that the Athenians decreed him a golden crown, and on account of his approved integrity, deposited the keys of their citadel in his hands. Antigouus Gonates, King of Macedon, was a constant attendant at his lectures while at Athens, and when that monarch returned, he earnestly invited Zeno to his court. During the philosopher's lifetime, the Athenians erected a statue of brass as a mark of the esteem in which they held him.

In person, Zeno was tall and slender; his brow was furrowed with thought; and this, with his long and close application to study, gave a tinge of severity to his aspect. Although of a feeble constitution, he preserved his health by his great abstention, his diet consisting of figs, bread, and honey. He was plain and modest in his dress and habits and very frugal in all his expenses, showing the same respect for the poor as for the rich, and conversing as freely with the slave as he did with the king.

His thought appears to have been an attempt to reconcile and combine what was very best in the theories of his day into one system. Taking from so many schools various portions of their doctrine, he seems to have provoked the antagonism of many of his contemporaries, and several philosophers of learning and ability employed their eloquence to diminish the growing influence of his new school. Towards the close of his life, he found a powerful antagonist in the person of Epicurus, and the Epicureans and Stoics have since treated each other as rival sects.

Zeno's school was generally a resort for the poor and it was a common joke among his adversaries that poverty was the charm for which he was indebted to his scholars. The list of his disciples, however, contains the names of some very rich and powerful men who may have regarded the Stoic theory as a powerful counteragent to the growing effeminacy of their age. After Zeno's death, around 265 B.C., the Athenians erected a monument to his memory.

Concerning philosophy in general, the doctrine of the Stoics was, that wisdom consists in the knowledge of things divine and human; that philosophy is such an exercise of the mind as produces wisdom; that in this exercise consists the nature of virtue; and consequently, that virtue is a term of extensive meaning, comprehending the right employment of the mind in reasoning, in the study of nature, and in morals. The wisdom of the Stoics is either progressive, through several stages; or perfect, when every weakness if subdued, and every error corrected, without the possibility of a relapse into folly, or vice, or of being again enslaved by any passion, or afflicted by any calamity.

With Socrates and the Cynics, Zeno represented virtue as the only true wisdom; but being disposed to extend the pursuits of his wise man into the regions of speculation and science, he gave, after his usual manner, a new signification to an old term, and comprehended the exercise of the understanding in the search of truth, as well as the government of the appetites and passions, under the general term, virtue. The great importance of the united exercise of the intellectual and active powers of the mind, are thus beautifully asserted by Marcus Aurelius.

> *Let everyone endeavor so to think and act, so that his contemplative and active faculties may at the same time be going on towards perfection. His clear conceptions, and certain knowledge, will then produce within him an entire confidence in himself, unperceived perhaps by others, though not affectedly concealed, which will give a simplicity and dignity to his character; for he will at all times*

be able to judge, concerning the several objects which come before him, what is their real nature, what place they hold in the universe, how long they are by nature fitted to last, of what materials they are composed, by whom they may be possessed, and who is able to bestow them, or take them away.

Let us pass on to the Stoic doctrine concerning Nature. According to Zeno and his followers, there existed from eternity a dark and confused chaos, in which was contained the first principles of all future beings. This chaos being at length arranged, and emerging into variable forms, became the world, as it now subsists. The world, or Nature, is that whole which comprehends all things, and of which all things are parts and members. The universe, though one whole, contains two principles, distinct from elements, one passive, the other active. The passive principle is pure matter without qualities; the active principle is reason, or logos. This is the fundamental doctrine of the Stoics concerning Nature.

The Stoic system teaches that both the active and passive principles in Nature are corporeal, since whatever acts or suffers must be so. The efficient cause, or logos, is pure ether, or fire, inhabiting the exterior surface of the heavens, where everything which is divine is placed. This ethereal substance, or divine fire, comprehends all the vital principles by which individual beings are necessarily produced, and contains the forms of things, which from the highest regions of the universe, are diffused through every other part of Nature. Seneca, indeed, calls logos incorporeal reason; but by this term he can only mean to distinguish the divine ethereal substance from gross bodies; for, according to the Stoics, whatever has a substantial existence is corporeal; nothing is incorporeal, except that infinite vacuum which surrounds the universe.

Matter, or the passive principle, in the Stoical system, is destitute of all qualities, but ready to receive any form, inactive, and without motion, unless moved by some external cause. The contrary principle, or logos, being active like an ethereal operative fire, and capable of producing all things from matter, with consummate skill, according to the forms which it contains, although in its nature corporeal, considered in opposition to gross and sluggish matter, or to the elements, is said to be immaterial and spiritual. For want of carefully attending to the preceding distinction, some writers have been so far imposed upon, by the bold innovations of the Stoics in the use of terms, as to infer from the appellations which they sometimes apply to the Deity, that they conceived him to be strictly and properly incorporeal. The truth appears to be, that, as they sometimes spoke of the soul of man, a portion of the divinity, as an exceedingly rare and subtle body, and sometimes as a warm or fiery spirit, so they spoke of the Deity as corporeal, considered as distinct from the incorporeal vacuum, or infinite space; but as spiritual, considered in opposition to gross and inactive matter. They taught, indeed, that logos is underived, incorruptible, and eternal, possessed of intelligence, good and perfect, the efficient cause of all the peculiar qualities or forms of things; and the constant preserver and governor of the world; and they described the

Deity under many noble images, and in the most elevated language.

What notions the Stoics entertained of logos sufficiently appears from the single opinion of its finite nature; an opinion which necessarily followed from the notion that it is only a part of a spherical, and therefore a finite universe. On the doctrine of divine providence, which was one of the chief points upon which the Stoics disputed with the Epicureans, much is written, and with great strength and elegance, by Seneca, Epictetus, and other later Stoics. But we are not to judge of the genuine and original doctrine of this sect from the discourses of these writers. The only way to form an accurate judgment of their opinions concerning providence is to compare their popular language upon this subject with their general system and explain the former consistently with the fundamental principles of the latter. If this be fairly done, it will appear that the agency of Deity is, according to the Stoics, logos which is the active motion of a celestial ether, or fire, possessed of intelligence, which at first gave form to the shapeless mass of gross matter, and being always essentially united to the visible world by the same necessary agency, preserves its order and harmony.

The Stoic idea of providence is, not that of a being, wholly independent of matter, freely directing and governing all things, but that of a necessary chain of causes and effects, arising from the actions of logos, which is itself a part of the existence which it regulates, and which equally with that existence is subject to the immutable law of necessity. Providence, in the Stoic creed, is only another name for absolute necessity, or fate, to which logos and matter, or the universe, which consists of both, is immutably subject. The rational, efficient, and active principle in Nature, the Stoics called by various names: logos, Nature, or fate. "What is Nature," says Seneca, "but logos; the divine reason, inherent in the whole universe, and in all its parts? Or you may call it, if you please, the author of all things."

And again: "Whatever appellations imply celestial power and energy, may be justly applied to logos; its names may properly be as numerous as its offices," The term "Nature," when it is at all distinguished in the Stoic system from logos, denotes not a separate agent, but that order of things which is necessarily produced by its perpetual agency. Since the active principle of Nature is comprehended within the world, and with matter makes one whole, it necessarily follows that logos penetrates, pervades, and animates matter, and the things which are formed from it, including ultimately human beings, or, in other words, that logos is the soul of the universe.

The universe is, according to Zeno and his followers, "a sentient and animated being." Nor was this a new tenet, but, in some sort, the doctrine of all antiquity. Pythagoras, Heraclitus, and after these, Zeno, taking it for granted that there is no real existence which is not corporeal, conceived Nature to be one whole, consisting of a subtle ether and gross matter, the former the active, the latter the passive principle, as essentially united as the soul and body of man that is, they supposed logos, with respect to Nature, to be, not a co-existing, but an informing principle.

Concerning the second principle in the universe, matter, and concerning the visible world, the doctrine of the Stoics is briefly this: Matter is the first essence of all things, destitute of, but capable of receiving, qualities. Considered universally, it is an eternal whole, which neither increases nor decreases. Considered with respect to its parts, it is capable of increase or diminution, of collision and separation, and is perpetually changing. Bodies are continually tending towards dissolution; matter always remains the same. Matter is not infinite, but finite, being circumscribed by the limits of the world; but its parts are infinitely divisible. The world is spherical in its form; and is surrounded by an infinite vacuum. The action of the divine nature upon matter first produced the element of moisture, and then the other elements, fire, air, and earth, of which all bodies are composed. Air and fire have essential levity or tend towards the exterior surface of the world; earth and water have essential gravity, or tend towards the centre. All the elements are capable of reciprocal conversion; air passing into fire, or into water; earth into air and water; but there is this essential difference among the elements, that fire and air have within themselves a principle of motion, while water and earth are merely passive.

The world, including the whole of Nature, logos and matter, subsisted from eternity, and will forever subsist; but the present regular frame of Nature had a beginning, and will have an end. The parts tend towards a dissolution, but the whole remains immutably the same. The world is liable to destruction from the prevalence of moisture, or of dryness; the former producing a universal inundation, the latter a universal conflagration. These succeed each other in Nature as regularly as winter and summer. When the universal inundation takes place, the whole surface of the earth is covered with water, and all animal life is destroyed; after which, Nature is renewed and subsists as before, till the element of fire, becoming prevalent in its turn, dries up all the moisture, converts every substance into its own nature, and at last, by a universal conflagration, reduces the world to its pristine state. At this period, all material forms are lost in one chaotic mass, all animated nature is re-united to the Deity, and Nature again exists in its original form, as one whole, consisting of logos and matter. From this chaotic state, however, it again emerges, by the energy of the efficient principle and all the forms of its regulated nature, only to be dissolved and renewed in endless succession.

Certainly, at this point something should be said about the relationship between Stoic thought and Christian theology. For, as we saw previously, Stoic thought has in it the idea, just as the Book of Genesis does, that the creation of the world comes in the form of a bringing of chaos to order. And Stoic thought also has in it the idea of a great flood, as does the Book of Genesis, and a universal conflagration, as does the Book of Revelation. Plus, the very Greek term "logos" (often translated "Word") is also used to describe this ordering force of creation in the very first sentence of the Gospel of John!

Further, in the area of Spirituality, Stoicism contains within it an idea which seems to suggest the existence of a sort of divine providence (just as Christianity does).

Therefore, to anyone even somewhat curious, the question naturally arises, "What can be said of these interesting parallels between Stoicism and Christianity?"

Certainly, from a practical perspective, they suggest that Stoicism, which is in fact an earlier school of thought than Christianity, should, at the very least, draw the interest of the average Christian. Perhaps, if for no other reason, as evidence that the "fullness of time" for the coming of Jesus (Galatians 4:4) is in some way related to these many parallel, yet still imperfect, ideas of the Stoics. And this thought might lead to the even greater inspiration that in order to fully understand Christianity a certain study of Classical Greek Philosophy is in fact called for. In this way true Stoic thought, not the almost complete misrepresentation we get of it in popular culture, represents a sort of natural motivation for those interested in faith to also study reason. And this can only produce good results and is, in fact, actually called for by Pope John Paul II in his fine encyclical <u>Fides et Ratio</u> (Faith and Reason).

The Stoic doctrine regarding the nature of mankind is also worthy of note. For in the same way as the logos is in the universe the logos is also in each individual human being. And the fact that, for the Stoics, this divine ordering force of logos pervades all things leads to one of the greatest of all noble thoughts— that all human beings have a special dignity which is expressed in the Stoic idea that there is a spark of the divine within each one of us.

And since the same logos which is in man is also in the universe the latter is no longer seen as some sort of a great unknown dark force which must be appeased, as many of the ancients did indeed see it, but as something that contains beauty and order and can in fact be known by man. And what idea is more fundamental to scientific thought than this? That if things are studied, they can in fact be known!

Thus the Stoics, in terms of both human dignity and scientific thought, present to us a great and truly foundational expression of freethinking!

EPICURUS

Epicurus was born in the early part of the year 344, B. C, the third year of the 109th Olympiad, at Gargettus, in the neighborhood of Athens. His father, Neocles, was of the Aegean tribe. Some allege that Epicurus was born on the island of Samos; but, according to others, he was taken there when very young by his parents, who formed a portion of a colony of Athenian citizens, sent to colonize Samos after its subjugation by Pericles. The father and mother of Epicurus were in very humble circumstances; his father was a schoolmaster, and his mother, Chrestrata, acted as a kind of priestess, curing diseases, exorcising ghosts, and exercising other fabulous powers. Epicurus has been charged with sorcery, because he wrote several songs for his mother's solemn rites. Until eighteen, he remained at Samos and the neighboring isle of Teos; from where he removed to Athens, where he resided until the death of Alexander, when, disturbances arising, he fled to Colophon. This place, Mitylene, and Lampsacus, formed the philosopher's residence until he was thirty-six years of age;

at which time he founded a school in the neighborhood of Athens. He purchased a pleasant garden, where he taught his disciples until the time of his death.

We are told by Laertius that those disciples who were regularly admitted into the school of Epicurus, lived together, not in the manner of the Pythagoreans, who cast their possessions into a common stock; for this, in his opinion, implied mutual distrust rather than friendship; but upon such a footing of friendly attachment, that each individual cheerfully supplied the necessities of his brother.

The habits of the philosopher and his followers were temperate and exceedingly frugal, and formed a strong contrast to the luxurious, although refined, manners of the Athenians and the common stereotypical understanding of them even today. For at the entrance of the garden, the visitor of Epicurus found the following inscription:

*The hospitable keeper of this mansion, where
you will find pleasure the highest good, will*

present you with barley cakes and water from the spring. These gardens will not provoke your appetite by artificial dainties but satisfy it with natural supplies. Will you not, then, be well entertained?

And yet the owner of the garden, over the gate of which these words were placed, has been called "a glutton" and "a stomach worshipper!"

From the age of thirty-six until his death, he does not seem to have left Athens, except temporarily. When Demetrius besieged Athens, the Epicureans were driven into great difficulties for want of food; and it is said that Epicurus and his friends subsisted on a small quantity of beans which he possessed, and which he shared equally with them.

The better to prosecute his studies, Epicurus lived a life of celibacy. Temperate and continent himself, he taught his followers to be so likewise, both by example and precept. He died in 273 B. C, in the seventy-third year of his age; and, at that time, his warmest opponents seem to have paid the highest compliments to his personal character; and, on reading his life, and the detailed accounts of his teachings, it seems difficult to imagine what has induced the scandal which has been heaped upon his memory.

We cannot quote from his own works, in his own words, because, although he wrote much, only a summary of his writings has come to us uninjured; but his doctrines have been so fully investigated and treated on, both by his opponents and his disciples, that there is no difficulty or doubt as to the principles inculcated in the school of Epicurus.

Philosophy for Epicurus is the exercise of reason in the pursuit and attainment of a happy life; where it follows, that those studies which conduce neither to the acquisition nor the enjoyment of happiness are to be dismissed as of no value at all. The end of all speculation ought to be, to enable men to judge with certainty what is to be chosen, and what to be avoided, to preserve themselves free from pain, and to secure health of body, and tranquility of mind. True philosophy is so useful to every man, that the young should apply to it without delay, and the old should never be weary of the pursuit of it; for no man is either too young or too old to correct and improve his mind, and to study the art of happiness.

Happy are they who possess by nature a free and vigorous intellect, and who are born into a country where they can prosecute their inquiries without restraint. For it is philosophy alone which raises a man above vain fears and base passions and gives him the perfect command of himself. Nothing ought to be dearer to a philosopher than truth. He should pursue it by the most direct means devising no actions himself, nor suffering himself to be imposed upon by others, neither poets, orators, nor logicians, making no other use of the rules of rhetoric or grammar, than to enable him to speak or write with accuracy and clarity, and always preferring a plain and simple to an ornamented style. While some doubt of everything, and others profess to know everything, a wise man will embrace only such tenets as are built upon experience, or upon certain and indisputable axioms.

The following is a summary of his Moral Philosophy:

The end of living, or the ultimate good, which is to be sought for its own sake, according to the universal opinion of mankind, is happiness; yet men, for the most part, fail in the pursuit of this end, either because they do not form a right idea of the nature of happiness, or because they do not make use of the proper means to attain it. Since it is every man's interest to be happy through the whole of life, it is wise to employ philosophy in the search of happiness without delay; and there cannot be a greater folly, than to be always beginning to live.

The happiness which belongs to man, is that state in which he enjoys as many of the good things, and suffers as few of the evils incident to human nature as possible; passing his days in a smooth course of permanent tranquility. A wise man, though deprived of sight or hearing, may experience happiness in the enjoyment of the good things which yet remain; and when suffering torture, or laboring under some painful disease, can mitigate the anguish by patience, and can enjoy, in his afflictions, the consciousness of his own constancy. But it is impossible that perfect happiness can be possessed without the pleasure which attends freedom from pain, and the enjoyment of the good things of life.

Pleasure is in its nature good, as pain is in its nature evil; the one is, therefore, to be pursued, and the other to be avoided, for its own sake. Pleasure, or pain, is not only good, or evil, in itself, but the measure of what is good or evil, in every object of desire or aversion; for the ultimate reason why we pursue one thing, and avoid another, is because we expect pleasure from the former, and pain from the latter.

If we sometimes decline a present pleasure, it is not because we are averse to pleasure itself, but because we conceive, that in the present instance, it will be necessarily connected with a greater pain. In like manner, if we sometimes voluntarily submit to a present pain, it is because we judge that it is necessarily connected with a greater pleasure.

Although all pleasure is essentially good, and all pain essentially evil, it does not then necessarily follow, that in every single instance the one ought to be pursued, and the other to be avoided; but reason is to be employed in distinguishing and comparing the nature and degrees of each, that the result may be a wise choice of that which shall appear to be, upon the whole, good.

That pleasure is the first good, appears from the inclination which every animal, from its first birth, discovers to pursue pleasure, and avoid pain; and is confirmed by the universal experience of mankind, who are incited to action by no other principle than the desire of avoiding pain, or obtaining pleasure. There are two kinds of pleasure: one consisting in a state of rest, in which both body and mind are undisturbed by any kind of pain; the other arising from an agreeable agitation of the senses, producing a correspondent emotion in the soul. It is upon the former of these that the enjoyment of life chiefly depends. Happiness may therefore be said to consist of bodily ease, and mental tranquility.

When pleasure is asserted to be the end of living, we are not then to understand that violent kind of delight or joy which arises from the gratification of the senses and passions, but merely that placid state of mind, which results from the absence of every cause of pain or uneasiness. Those pleasures, which arise from agitation, are not to be pursued as the end of living, but as a means of arriving at that stable tranquility, in which true happiness consists. It is the office of reason to confine the pursuit of pleasure within the limits of nature, in order to the attainment of that happy state, in which the body is free from every kind of pain, and the mind from all perturbation. This state must not, however, be conceived to be perfect in proportion as it is inactive, but in proportion as all the functions of life are quietly and pleasantly performed. A happy life neither resembles a rapid torrent, nor a standing pool, but is like a gentle stream, that glides smoothly and silently along.

This happy state can only be obtained by a prudent care of the body, and a steady government of the mind. The diseases of the body are to be prevented by temperance, or cured by medicine, or rendered tolerable by patience. Against the diseases of the mind, philosophy provides sufficient antidotes. The instruments which it employs for this purpose are the virtues; the root of which, when all the rest proceeds, is prudence. This virtue comprehends the whole art of living discreetly, justly, and honorably, and is, in fact, the same thing as wisdom. It instructs men to free their understandings from the clouds of prejudice; to exercise temperance and fortitude in the government of themselves: and to practice justice towards others. Although pleasure, or happiness, which is the end of living, be superior to virtue, which is only the means, it is every one's interest to practice all the virtues; for in a happy life, pleasure can never be separated from virtue.

A prudent man, in order to secure his tranquility, will consult his natural disposition in the choice of his plan of life. If, for example, he is persuaded that he should be happier in a state of marriage than in celibacy, he ought to marry; but if he be convinced that matrimony would be an impediment to his happiness, he ought to remain single. In like manner, such persons as are naturally active, enterprising, and ambitious, or such as by the condition of their birth are placed in the way of civil offices, should accommodate themselves to their nature and situation, by engaging in public affairs; while such as are, from natural temper, fond of leisure and retirement, or, from experience or observation, are convinced that a life of public business would be inconsistent with their happiness, are unquestionably at liberty, except where particular circumstances call them to the service of their country, to pass their lives in obscure repose.

Temperance is that discreet regulation of desires and passions, by which we are enabled to enjoy pleasures without suffering any consequent inconvenience. They who maintain such a constant self-command, as never to be enticed by the prospect of present indulgence, to do that which will be productive of evil, obtain the truest pleasure by declining pleasure. Since, of desires some are natural and necessary; others natural, but not necessary; and others neither natural nor necessary, but the offspring of false judgment; it must be the office of temperance to gratify the first class, as far as nature requires: to restrain the second within the bounds of moderation; and, as to the third, resolutely to oppose, and, if possible, entirely repress them.

Sobriety, as opposed to inebriety and gluttony, is of admirable use in teaching men that nature is satisfied with a little and enabling them to content themselves with simple and frugal fare. Such a manner of living is conducive to the preservation of health renders a man alert and active in all the offices of life; affords him an exquisite relish of the occasional varieties of a plentiful board, and prepares him to meet every reverse of fortune without the fear of want.

Continence is a branch of temperance, which prevents the diseases, infamy, remorse, and punishment, to which those who are exposed, who indulge themselves in unlawful lusts. Music and poetry, which are often employed as incentives to licentious pleasure are to be cautiously and sparingly used.

Gentleness, as opposed to an irascible temper, greatly contributes to the tranquility and happiness of life, by preserving the mind from perturbation, and arming it against the assaults of calumny and malice. A wise man, who puts himself under the government of reason, will be able to receive an injury with calmness, and to treat the person who committed it with lenity; for he will rank injuries among the casual events of life, and will prudently reflect that he can no more stop the natural current of human passions, than he can curb the stormy winds.

Moderation in the pursuit of honors and riches is the only security against vexation and disappointment. A wise man prefers the simplicity of the rustic life to the magnificence of the courts. A wise man considers the future as uncertain and will neither be elated with confident expectation or depressed by doubt and despair. It contributes to the enjoyment of life to consider death as the perfect end of a happy life, which we should close like satisfied guests, neither regretting the past, nor anxious for the future.

Fortitude, the virtue which enables us to endure pain and to banish fear, is of great use in producing tranquility. Philosophy instructs us to pay homage to the gods, not through hope or fear, but from veneration of their superior nature. It moreover enables us to conquer the fear of death, by teaching us that it is no proper object of terror; since, while we are, death is not, and when death arrives, we are not: so that it neither concerns the living nor the dead.

The only evils to be avoided are bodily pain, and distress of mind. Bodily pain should be endured by a wise man with patience and firmness; because, if it be slight, it may easily be borne; and if it be intense, it cannot last long. Mental distress commonly arises not from nature but from opinion. A wise man will therefore arm himself against this kind of suffering by reflecting that the gifts of fortune, the loss of which he may be inclined to deplore, were never his own but dependent upon circumstances which he could not command. Therefore, if they happen to leave him, he will endeavor to obliterate their remembrance by occupying his mind in pleasant contemplation and engaging in agreeable avocations.

Justice respects man as living in society and is the common bond without which no society can subsist. This virtue, like the rest, derives its value from its tendency to promote the happiness of life. Not only is it never injurious to the man who practices it but nourishes-in his mind calm reflections and pleasant hopes; whereas it is impossible that the mind in which injustice dwells, should not be full of disquietude. Since it is impossible that iniquitous actions should promote the enjoyment of life, as much as remorse of conscience, legal penalties, and public disgrace, must increase its troubles, everyone who follows the dictates of sound reason, will practice the virtues of justice, equity, and fidelity.

In society, the necessity of the mutual exercise of justice, in order to the common enjoyment of the gifts of nature, is the ground of those laws by which it is prescribed. It is in the interest of every individual in a state to conform to the laws of justice; for by injuring no one, and rendering to every man his due, he contributes his part towards the preservation of that society, upon the perpetuity of which his own safety depends. Nor ought any one to think that he is at liberty to violate the rights of his fellow citizens, provided he can do it securely; for he who has committed an unjust act can never be certain that it will not be discovered; and however successfully he may conceal it from others, this will avail him little, since he can never conceal it from himself. In different communities, different laws may be instituted, according to the circumstances of the people who compose them. Whatever is then prescribed is to be considered as a rule of justice, so long as society shall judge the observance of it to be for the benefit of the whole. But whenever any rule of conduct is found not to be conducive to the public good it should no longer be prescribed.

Nearly allied to justice are the virtues of beneficence, compassion, gratitude, piety, and friendship. He who confers benefits upon others, procures to himself the satisfaction of seeing the stream of plenty spreading around him from the fountain of his beneficence; at the same time, he enjoys the pleasure of being esteemed by others. The exercise of gratitude, filial affection, and reverence for the gods, is necessary, in order to avoid the hatred and contempt of all men.

Friendships are contracted for the sake of mutual benefit; but by degrees they ripen into such disinterested attachment, that they are continued without any prospect of advantage. Between friends there is a kind of league, that each will love the other as himself. A true friend will partake of the wants and sorrows of his friend, as if they were his own; if he be in want, he will relieve him; if he be in prison, he will visit him; if he be sick, he will come to him; situations may even occur, in which he would not hesitate to die for him. It cannot then be doubted, that friendship is one of the most useful means of procuring a secure, tranquil, and happy life.

No man will find anything in the foregoing summary to justify the foul language used against Epicurus, and his moral philosophy; the secret is in the physical doctrines, and this secret is, that Epicurus was actually, if not intentionally, a Materialist. The following is a summary of his physical doctrine:

Nothing can spring from nothing, nor can anything return to nothing. The universe always existed and will always remain; for there is nothing into which it can be changed. There is nothing in Nature, nor can anything be conceived, besides body and space. Body is that which possesses the properties of bulk, figure, resistance, and gravity. It is this alone which can touch or be touched. Space is the region which is occupied by body, and which affords it an opportunity of moving freely. That there are bodies in the universe is attested to by the senses. That there is also space is evident; since otherwise bodies would have no place in which to move or exist, and of their existence and motion we have the proof of perception. Besides these, no third nature can be conceived; for such a nature must either have bulk and solidity, or want them; that is, it must either be body or space: this does not, however, preclude the existence of qualities which have no subsistence.

The universe, consisting of body and space, is infinite, for it has no limits. Bodies are infinite in multitude; space is infinite in magnitude. The term above, or beneath, high or low, cannot be properly applied to infinite space. The universe is to be conceived as immoveable, since beyond it there is no place into which it can move; and as eternal and immutable, since it is neither liable to increase nor decrease, to production nor decay. Nevertheless, the parts of the universe are in motion, and are subject to change.

All bodies consist of parts, of which they are composed, and into which they may be resolved; and these parts are either themselves simple principles or may be resolved into such. These first principles, or simple atoms, are divisible by no force, and, therefore, must be immutable. This may also be inferred from the uniformity of Nature, which could not be preserved if its principles were not certain and consistent. The existence of such atoms is evident, since it is impossible that anything which exists should be reduced to nothing. A finite body cannot consist of parts infinite, either in magnitude or number; divisibility of bodies ad infinitum, is therefore conceivable. All atoms are of the same nature or differ in no essential qualities. From their different effects upon the senses, it appears, however, that they differ in magnitude, figure, and weight. Atoms exist in every possible variety of figure: round, oval, conical, cubical, sharp, hooked, etc. But in every shape, they are, on account of their solidity, infrangible, or incapable of actual division.

Gravity must be an essential property of atoms; for since they are perpetually in motion, or making an effort to move, they must be moved by an internal impulse, which may be called gravity. The principle of gravity, that internal energy which is the cause of all motion, whether simple or complex, being essential to the primary corpuscles or atoms, they must have been incessantly and from eternity in actual motion.

Epicurus was a materialist who held that the only reliable evidence was that of the senses. Therefore, in a theoretical sense, one would not expect that he would be favorably disposed to the concept of God (or the gods).

However, in an ethical sense, Epicurus rightly understood that the question of happiness could not be resolved without dealing, to one extent or another, with the question of God. He thus came up with one of the most interesting and unique attitudes toward the gods of any philosopher.

In his "Letter to Menoeceus" he states:

> *First of all, believe that god is a being immortal and blessed… believe about him everything that can uphold his blessedness and immortality. For gods there are, since the knowledge of them is by clear vision. But they are not such as the many believe them to be.*

However, he goes on to conclude that:

> *Become accustomed to the fact that death is nothing to us: For all good and evil consist in sensation: but death is deprivation of sensation.*

Here Epicurus displays both a keen social psychology and a great theoretical integrity. For he knows well from the beginning that his system can have no place for an afterlife, yet he also knows that to deny the gods would create a conflict both within the mind of the average man, and between him and his fellow men. So, almost like giving to Caesar what is due to Caesar and to God what is due to God, Epicurus gives the gods their due yet calmly points out that in the end "death is nothing to us." And in this many current day militant atheists and agnostics can learn a great lesson.

If we attempt to review the teachings of Epicurus we see that some are defective and imperfect in many respects. This is necessarily so because the imperfect science of the day limited the array of facts presented to him. Therefore, the structure is weak in many points because it was too large for its own foundation. However, we would be wise not to pass on it but rather make it our own task to lay a good, wide, and sure foundation on which to build up this system which after all has for its end the happiness of all mankind.

In closing, it is important to note that although the instruction of Epicurus to obtain the greatest amount of pleasure and the least amount of pain for oneself may seem self-serving it is in fact in line with the Christian teaching that one should love your neighbor as you love yourself. For in both teachings is contained the idea that the effective love of self leads to the effective love of others.

In this way, the freethinking of Epicurus serves as a guide not only to the later Utilitarian philosophy of Bentham and Mill, which it in fact directly inspired, but to that highest expression of Ethics put forth in the Golden Rule of Jesus of Nazareth!

AVERROES

Averroes was born in Cordoba, Spain in 1126 A.D. Highly skilled in law, philosophy, theology, medicine, and many other arts Averroes came from a noble family in which both his grandfather and father had served as the chief judge of Cordoba.

Ironically, Averroes' greatest contributions have perhaps been to the West rather than to the East, and to Christianity rather than to Islam. And the very fact that he is at the same time considered the founding father of secular Europe and, because of his commentaries on Aristotle, a key figure in the Scholastic movement shows the depth of his credentials as one of history's great freethinkers.

The Internet Encyclopedia of Philosophy states the following about the influence of Averroes.

> *His influential commentaries and unique interpretations on Aristotle revived Western scholarly interest in ancient Greek philosophy, whose works for the most part had been*

neglected since the sixth century. He critically examined the alleged tension between philosophy and religion in the "Decisive Treatise" and he challenged the anti-philosophical sentiments within the Sunni tradition sparked by al-Ghazzali. This critique ignited a similar re-examination within the Christian tradition, influencing a line of scholars who would come to be identified as the "Averroists."

Averroes was particularly skilled in medicine yet particularly interested in the relationship between theology and philosophy (or faith and reason). Although he has been called a rationalist his position on the search for truth is actually much more subtle. Averroes held that there is no conflict between theology and philosophy and that they are rather just two different ways of reaching religious truth. The first being the way of faith and the second being the way of reason. Philosophy, as the higher path, being reserved for those learned who have the good fortune to study it. In his work <u>The Exposition</u> he says of this relationship:

In a separate treatise, we have already dealt with the harmony of philosophy and religion, indicating how religion commands the study of philosophy. We maintained there that religion consists of two part: external and interpreted, and that the external part is incumbent on the masses, whereas the interpreted is incumbent on the learned.

The work referred to here is <u>The Decisive Treatise</u>. In it Averroes lays out the proper way for philosophical or logical methods to be used in religious controversies. He starts by defining philosophy as "The investigation of existing entities in so far as they point to the maker." Averroes then goes on to claim that sacred scripture itself calls for the use of philosophy in such interpretation when, in Qur'anic verses such as 59:2, it urges people of understanding to reflect and, in verse 7:184, it asks believers to use reason and intellect. For these reasons Averroes contends that the claims of some Muslim theologians that philosophy is useless to religion are not only false, but are in fact contrary to sacred scripture itself!

In this way Averroes begins to show his ability for critical exegesis of Quranic verses. Yet this exegesis is limited both in terms of who is qualified to engage in it and in which scriptures might be interpreted. Averroes holds that the statements of scripture which are explicit do not call for any interpretation but that the statements of scripture which are ambiguous should be interpreted, yet only by the learned. And that, further, the learned should not share these interpretations with the masses but only among their own class.

Averroes holds that there are three ways of arriving at religious truth, and that philosophy, as the best of these ways, should not be prohibited. In explaining the three ways Averroes points out that any religion which posits a universal acceptance must present its message in a suitable form for all. And that the learned will be attracted to Islam by philosophical arguments, the theologians will be attracted by an understand of parables, and the common people, who are not capable of such understandings, will be attracted by rhetorical devices which include some logic yet mainly rely on imagery and exhortation.

Averroes also challenged various versions of Islamic theology noting that certain issues arising out of their notions of occasionalism, divine speech, and explanations of the origin of the world could not be explained in depth without engaging in the critical thinking that only philosophy can bring. He went on to claim that without philosophy deeper meanings of Islam might ultimately be lost leading to many deviant and incorrect understandings of Islamic theology (and, given the situation of our own day, he was certainly quite prophetic in this).

It is worth noting what an amazing piece of freethinking this is. The idea that religious truth can be found not just by theology but also by philosophy was a radical, and perhaps quite dangerous, one for an Islamic scholar to hold. Yet Averroes brought it forth and held to it even in the face of his falling out of favor politically and eventually being banished. The implications of this idea are indeed radical. For if one can study philosophy rather than practice religion and still come to the same truths a radical rethinking of society, and in particular education, is in order. And it is indeed such a radical rethinking that has, along with other factors, produced modern secular Europe and modern secular public universities.

I often comment to my students at our modern secular public university in the United States that the public university classroom is one of the most sacred places in our society. For within its walls we are allowed to pursue truth freely because of the concept of Academic Freedom. Yet who do we ultimately owe this freedom to if not Averroes? For his insistence that reason is perhaps an even better path to truth than faith opened up the possibility for the free inquiry we still enjoy today.

Yet Averroes has also had a tremendous impact on Christianity. This is because Averroes was "The Commentator" on "The Philosopher" himself Aristotle. And these very terms "The Commentator" and "The Philosopher" were coined by none other than the great Catholic scholar Saint Thomas

Aquinas. For much of what Aquinas learned about Aristotle in the thirteenth century is due to the commentaries Averroes wrote on him in the twelfth. The New World Encyclopedia says of Averroes' role in the transmission of Aristotle's thought:

> *Averroes wrote three versions of his commentaries on Aristotle, known as the Minor, the Middle, and the Major commentaries… The Major commentaries were largely original. Averroes' commentaries do not provide a literal translation of Aristotle's works; since Averroes did not know Greek, he used an imperfect Arab translation of the Syriac version of the Greek text. The Commentaries do, however, contain detailed philosophical and scientific interpretations of Aristotle's thought.*

Before 1150 A.D. only a few translated works of Aristotle existed in Europe, and they did not receive a great deal of attention from monastic scholars. It was only through the Latin translations of Averroes' works, beginning in the twelfth century, that the legacy of Aristotle was recovered in the West by figures like Saint Thomas Aquinas.

A common theme between these two great thinkers is the relationship between faith and reason. Averroes held that both philosophy and theology were ways to truth—a radical idea in the Islam of his day. Although Christianity did have an existing tradition of faith and reason Aquinas was forced to defend it against many attacks ultimately perfecting the idea of the theological syllogism.

A syllogism is a form of argumentation invented by Aristotle yet transmitted to the West through the commentaries on him by Islamic scholars like Averroes. It is composed of several statements, known as premises, that are logically related. For example:

> *Major premise: All men are mortal*
> *Minor premise: Socrates is a man*
> *Conclusion: Socrates is mortal.*

In a normal syllogism the premises can be proven through observation and reason. However, in a theological syllogism this is sometimes not the case. What Aquinas points out, in the famous controversy on the topic at the University of Paris, is that although the premises of a theological syllogism sometimes cannot be proven by observation and reason they can in fact find their proofs in sacred scripture and tradition. Therefore, the new logic of Aristotle can be applied to theology in the form of the theological syllogism!

Thus a balance in the roles of reason and faith was struck in Christianity. And it is a balance which has remained to our own day. This is attested to in the encyclical of Pope John Paul II from 1998 entitled "Fides et Ratio" (Faith and Reason). For in it he states:

> *Faith and Reason are like two wings on which the human spirit rises to the contemplation of truth; and God has placed in the human heart a desire to know the truth— in a word, to know Himself—so that, by knowing and loving God, men and women may also come to the fullness of truth about themselves.*

The beautiful imagery of a bird rising to

the contemplation of the truth used by Pope John Paul II here is a clear message that it is only through a balance of faith and reason that a religion can thrive. For what can a bird with only one wing do besides spiral toward its own demise?

Thus Averroes, quite ironically, not only opened up the possibility for freethinking at secular universities but also provided Aquinas with the knowledge of Aristotelian Logic which was able to, at least for a time, defend the continued study of theology at the University of Paris.

And, remarkably enough, the fact that the University of Paris still had a theology department for a time (for it was closed during the French Revolution) later allowed Rene Descartes to dedicate his _Meditations on First Philosophy_ to "those most learned and distinguished men, the Dean and Doctors of the sacred Faculty of Theology at Paris" and open up the modern age. Thus here we see a direct connection between Averroes, Aquinas, and Descartes.

That this one relatively little known Islamic scholar has had such a profound impact on our history is indeed quite remarkable. Yet in a certain sense his story shows the power of freethinking like none other can. For this one brilliant freethinker has so changed the world with the power of his thought that his very name seems to have become overshadowed by his own achievements! Yet we can now know and celebrate him and be encouraged by the fact that Islam, too, is in the process of rediscovering him as well.

Perhaps the mark of this great freethinker on history has still not yet been fully made. For just as Averroes made his great contributions to the West and Christianity he still might have even greater contributions to make to his own people and tradition. Not the least of which might be an important understanding between Christianity and Islam about a shared heritage which now might become the basis for a common future. A common future lived out in peace, respect, and understanding.

RENE DESCARTES

Rene Descartes, the father of modern philosophy, was born at La Haye, in Touraine, of Breton parents, near the close of the sixteenth century, at a time when Francis Bacon was like the morning sun, rising to shed new rays of bright light over the then dark world of philosophy. The mother of Descartes died while he was but a few days old, and himself a sickly child, he began to take part in the battle of life with but little appearance of ever possessing the capability for action on the minds of his fellows, which he afterwards so fully exercised. Debarred, however, by his physical weakness from many boyish pursuits, he devoted himself to study in his earliest years, and during his youth gained the title of the young philosopher, from his eagerness to learn, and from his earnest endeavors by inquiry and experiment to solve every problem presented to his notice. He was educated in the Jesuits' College of La Fleche; and the monument erected to him at Stockholm informs us:

That having mastered all the learning of the schools, which proved short of his expectations, he betook himself to the army in Germany and Hungary, and there spent his vacant winter hours in comparing the mysteries and phenomena of nature with the laws of mathematics, daring to hope that the one might serve as a key to the other. Quitting, therefore, all other pursuits, he retired to a little village near Egmont, in Holland, where spending twenty-five years in continual reading and meditation, he effected his design.

In "Discourse on Method" he writes:

As soon as my age permitted me to leave my preceptors, I entirely gave up the study of letters; and, resolving to seek no other science than that which I could find in myself, or else in the great book of the world, I employed the remainder of my youth in travel—in seeing courts and camps—in frequenting people of diverse humors and conditions—in collecting various experiences; and, above all, in endeavoring to draw some profitable reflection from what I saw. For it seemed to me that I should meet with more truth in the reasoning which each man makes in his own affairs, and which, if wrong, would be speedily punished by failure, than in those reasoning which the philosopher makes in his study upon speculations which produce no effect, and which are of no consequence to him, except perhaps that he will be the more vain of them, the more remote they are from common sense, because he would then have been forced to employ more ingenuity and subtlety to render them plausible.

At the age of thirty-three Descartes retired from the world for a period of eight years. His seclusion was so effectual during that his place of residence was unknown to his friends. He there prepared the "Meditations," and "Discourse on Method," which have since caused so much controversy among those who aspired to be ranked as philosophical thinkers. He became famous all over Europe and was invited by Queen Christina of Sweden to visit her kingdom. However, the poor climate proved too much for his delicate frame, and he died at Stockholm in the year

1650, from inflammation of the lungs, being fifty-four years of age at the time of his death.

Descartes was perhaps the most original thinker that France had up to that date produced; and, contemporary with Bacon, he exercised a powerful influence or the progress of thought in Europe. And, despite any reports to the contrary, Descartes was supported in this effort in many ways by the Church. First, by the fact that he attended one of the greatest schools of his day which was founded and run by the Jesuits. Second, by the fact that one of his great friends and supporters was the Father Marin Mersenne. And third, by the fact that his most influential supporter was the Prince of the Church and spiritual writer Cardinal Pierre De Berulle.

Descartes gave a strong aid to the tendency of advancing modern civilization and to making a distinction between philosophy and theology. In his dedication of the "Meditations" he says:

> *I have always thought that the two questions of the existence of God and the nature of the*

soul, were the chief of those which ought to be demonstrated rather by philosophy than by theology; for although it is sufficient for us, the faithful, to believe in God, and that the soul does not perish with the body, it does not seem possible ever to persuade the Infidels to any religion, unless we first prove to them these two things by natural reason.

He thus sought a starting point from which to reason, some indisputable fact upon which to found future thinking.

At times lost in studies of Descartes are the radical methods he used in transmitting his thought. First, he wrote not in the scholarly Latin of his day but in the French spoken by the common man. Second, he wrote not in the distance third person but in a very personal first person style as a real man engaged in a real search for truth. In these ways Descartes brought the search for objective truth into the more subjective existence of everyday people. And that the Church eventually fully embraced these methods of Descartes is best seen in the fact that the Second Vatican Council essentially adopted both of these methods by insisting that the Mass, as much as was possible, be spoken in the common vernacular language rather than in scholarly Latin, and by teaching that everyday men in all walks of life, and not just clerics, are called to spread the Gospel into their own little part of the world. And in fully embracing Modernism the Church was, in fact, fully embracing Descartes.

Moving beyond Descartes' methods of transmission to the Meditations let us examine things more closely. Proceeding from the certainty of his existence, Descartes endeavors to find other equally certain facts, and for that purpose presents the following doctrine and rules for our guidance. The basis of all certitude is consciousness, consciousness is the sole foundation of absolute certainty, and whatever it distinctly proclaims must be true. The process is, therefore, rendered clear and simple: examine your consciousness—each distinct reply will be a fact.

He tells us further that all clear ideas are true. That whatever is clearly and distinctly conceived is true. And in these lie the vitality of his system, the cause of the truth or error of his thinking.

The following are his rules for detecting true ideas and separating false ones.

1. Never to accept anything as true but what is evidently so; to admit nothing but what so clearly and distinctly presents itself as true, that there can be no reason to doubt it.

2. To divide every question into as many separate parts as possible, that each part being more easily conceived, the whole may be more intelligible.

3. To conduct the examination with order, beginning by that of objects the most simple, and therefore the easiest to be known, and ascending little by little up to knowledge of the most complex.

4. To make such exact calculations, and such circumspections as to be confident that nothing essential has been omitted. Consciousness being the basis of all certitude, everything of which you are clearly and

distinctly conscious must be true, everything which you clearly and distinctly conceive, exists, if the idea of it involve existence.

In these four rules we have the essential part of one half of Descartes' system, the other, which is equally important, is the attempt to solve metaphysical problems by mathematical aid. To mathematics he had devoted much of his time. He it was who, at the age of twenty three, made the grand discovery of the applicability of algebra to geometry. While deeply engaged in mathematical studies and investigations, he came to the conclusion that mathematics were capable of a still further simplification, and of much more extended application. Impressed with the certainty of the conclusions arrived at by the aid of mathematical reasoning, he began to apply mathematics to metaphysics.

His ambition was to found a system which should be solid and convincing. Having searched for certitude, he had found its basis in consciousness; he next wanted a method, and hoped he had found it in mathematics. He tells us that:

Those long chains of reasoning, all simple and easy, by which geometers used to arrive at their most difficult demonstrations, suggested to him that all things which came within human knowledge, must follow each other in a similar chain; and that provided we abstain from admitting anything as true which is not so, and that we always preserve in them the order necessary to deduce one from the other, there can be none so remote to which we cannot finally attain, nor so obscure but that we may discover them.

Acting this out, he dealt with metaphysics like a problem from Euclid, and expected by rigorous reasoning to discover the truth. He, like Archimedes, sought a standing place from which to use the lever that should overturn the world. Finding this standing place in the indubitable fact of his own existence.

The Cartesian philosophy is founded on two great principles, the one metaphysical, the other physical. The metaphysical is Descartes' foundation-stone—the *"I think, therefore I am."* This has been warmly attacked as not being logical. Descartes said his existence was a fact—a fact above and beyond all logic; in that logic could neither prove nor disprove it. The was not new in itself, but it was the first stone of a new building—the first step in a new road: from this fact Descartes tried to reach another, and from that others.

The physical principle is that nothing exists but substance, which he makes of two kinds—the one a substance that thinks, the other a substance extended. Actual thought and actual extension are the essence of substance, so that the thinking substance cannot be without some actual thought, nor can anything be retrenched from the extension of a thing, without taking away so much of its actual substance.

Having formed his method, Descartes proceeded to apply it. The basis of certitude being consciousness, he interrogated his consciousness, and found that he had an idea of a substance infinite, eternal, immutable, independent, omniscient, omnipotent. This he called an idea of God: he said:

I exist as a miserably imperfect finite being, subject to change—ignorant, incapable of creating anything—I find by my finitude that I am not the infinite; by my liability to change that I am not the immutable; by my ignorance that I am not the omniscient: in short, by my imperfection, that I am not the perfect. Yet an infinite, immutable, omniscient, and perfect being must exist, because infinity, immutability, omniscience, and perfection are applied as correlatives in my ideas of finitude, change, etc. God therefore exists: his existence is clearly proclaimed in my consciousness, and therefore ceases to be a matter of doubt. The conception of an infinite being proved his real existence, for if there is not really such a being I must have made the conception; but if I could make it I can also unmake it, which evidently is not true; therefore there must be externally to myself, an archetype from which the conception was derived..... All that we clearly and distinctly conceive as contained in anything is true of that thing... Now, we conceive clearly and distinctly that the existence of God is contained in the idea we have of him: ergo—God exists.

Descartes was of opinion that his demonstrations of the existence of God "equal or even surpass in certitude the demonstrations of geometry."

Treating the existence of God as demonstrated from the a priori idea of perfection and infinity, and by the clearness of his idea of God's existence, Descartes then proceeds to deal with the distinction between body and soul. To prove this distinction was to him an easy matter. The fundamental and essential attribute of substance must be extension, because we can denude substance of every quality but that of extension; this we cannot touch without at the same time affecting the substance. The fundamental attribute of mind is thought; it is in the act of thinking that the consciousness of existence is revealed; to be without thought would be to be without consciousness.

Descartes has given us the axiom:

That two substances are really distinct when their ideas are complete, and no way imply each other. The idea of extension is complete and distinct from the idea of thought, which latter is also clear and distinct by itself. It follows, therefore, that substance and mind are distinct in essence.

Descartes has subjected himself to the charge of asserting the existence of innate ideas, and the following quotations will speak for themselves on the subject:

When I said that the idea of God is innate in us, I never meant more than this, that Nature has endowed us with a faculty by which we may know God; but I have never either said or thought that such ideas had an actual existence, or even that they were a species distinct from the faculty of thinking....
Although the idea of God is so imprinted on our minds, that every person has within him the faculty of knowing him, it does not follow that there may not have been various individuals who have passed through life without ever making this idea a distinct object of apprehension; and, in truth, they who think they have an idea of a plurality of Gods, have no idea of God whatever.

Descartes' disciples are of two classes, the "mathematical cultivators of physic," and the "deductive cultivators of philosophy." The first class of disciples are far in advance of their chief, and can only be considered as having received an impulse in a true direction. The second class unhesitatingly accepted his principles, and continued his thinking, although they developed his system in a different manner, and arrived at stronger conclusions than Descartes' courage would have supported. Some of the physical speculations of Descartes have been much ridiculed by subsequent writers; but many reasons may be urged, not only against that ridicule, but also against the more moderate censure which several able critics have dealt out against the intellectual character of Descartes. It should be remembered that the theories of all his predecessors were mere conjectural speculations respecting the places and paths of celestial bodies, etc. Innumerable hypotheses had been formed and found useless; and we ought rather to look to what Descartes did accomplish under the many difficulties of his position, in respect to the then, state of scientific knowledge, than to judge harshly of those speculations, which, though attended with no beneficial result to humanity at large, were doubtless well intended by their author.

He was the first man who brought optical science under the command of mathematics, by the discovery of the law of refraction of the ordinary ray through diaphanous bodies; and probably there is scarcely a name on record, the bearer of which has given a greater impulse to mathematical and philosophical inquiry than Descartes. Although, as a mathematician, he published but little, yet in every subject which he has treated he has opened, not only a new field for investigation, but also a new road for the investigators to proceed by. His discovery of the simple application of the notation of indices to algebraical powers, has totally remodeled the whole science of algebra. His conception of expressing the fundamental property of curve lines and curve surfaces by equations between the co-ordinates has led to an almost total supersedence of the geometry of the ancients.

We trust that in these few pages we have succeeded in presenting Descartes, to such of our readers who were unacquainted with his writings, sufficiently well to enable them to appreciate him, and to induce them to search further; and at the same time we hope that those better acquainted with him will not blame us for the omission of much which they may consider more important. We have endeavored to picture Descartes as the free thinking founder of a method, and as having the foundation-stone of all his reasoning in his freethinking consciousness.

BARUCH SPINOZA

Baruch Spinoza, or Espinoza, better known under the name of Benedict Spinoza (as rendered by himself in the Latin language,) was born at Amsterdam, in Holland, on the 24th of November, 1632. There is some uncertainty as to this date, as there are several dates fixed by different authors, both for his birth and death, but we have adopted the biography given by Dr. C. H. Bruder, in the preface to his edition of Spinoza's works. His parents were Jews of the middle, or, perhaps, somewhat humbler class. His father was originally a Spanish merchant, who, to escape persecution, had immigrated to Holland. Although the life of our great philosopher is one full of interesting incidents, and deserves to be treated fully, we have but room to give a very brief sketch, referring our readers, who may wish to learn more of Spinoza's life.

Spinoza appears in his boyhood to have been an apt scholar, and to have rapidly mastered the tasks set him by his teachers. Full of rabbinical lore he won the admiration of the Rabbi Moses Mortira, but the pupil rose higher than his master, and attempted to solve problems which the learned rabbis were content to reverence as mysteries not capable of solution. First they remonstrated, then threatened; still Spinoza persevered in his studies, and in making known the result to those around him. He was threatened with excommunication and withdrew himself from the synagogue.

In the year 1660, Spinoza, being then twenty-eight years of age, and an outcast from the home of his youth, gained a humble livelihood by polishing glasses for microscopes, telescopes, etc., at which he was very expert. While thus acquiring, by his own handiwork, the means of subsistence, he was studying hard, devoting every possible hour to philosophical research. Spinoza became master of the Dutch, Hebrew, German, Spanish, Portuguese, and Latin languages, the latter of which he acquired in the house of one Francis Van den Ende, from whom it is more than probable he received as much instruction in atheism as in Latin.

Spinoza only appears to have once fallen in love, and this was with Van den Ende's daughter, who was herself a good linguist, and who gave Spinoza instruction in Latin. She, however, although willing to be his instructress and companion in a philogical path, declined to accept his love, and thus Spinoza was left to philosophy alone.

He retired to Rhynsburg, near the City of Leyden, in Holland, and there studied the works of Descartes. Three years afterwards he published an abridgment of the "Meditations" of the great father of philosophy, which created a profound sensation. In an appendix to this abridgment were contained the germs of those thinking in which the pupil outdid the master, and the student progressed beyond the philosopher.

In the month of June, 1664, Spinoza removed to Woorburg, a small village near the Hague, where he was visited by persons from different parts, attracted by his fame as a philosopher; and at last, after many solicitations he came to the Hague, and resided there altogether. Spinoza died on the

21st or 22nd of February, 1677, in his forty-fifth year, and was buried on the 25th of February at the Hague. He was frugal in his habits, subsisting independently on the earnings of his own hands. Honorable in all things, he refused to accept the chair of Professor of Philosophy, offered to him by the Elector, and this because he did not wish to be circumscribed in his thinking, or in the freedom of utterance of his thoughts. He also refused a pension offered to him by Louis XIV, saying that he had no intention of dedicating anything to that monarch.

The "Tractatus Politicus" has been translated into English by William Maccall, who seems fully to appreciate the greatness of the philosopher, although he will not admit the usefulness of Spinoza's logic. Maccall does not see the utility of that very logic which compelled him to admit Spinoza's truth. We are not aware of any other translation of Spinoza's works except that of a small portion of his "Ethica," by Lewes. This work, which was originally published in 1677, commenced with eight definitions which are at this point worth reviewing.

DEFINITIONS.

I. By cause of itself I understand that, the essence of which involves existence: or that, the nature of which can only be considered as existent.

II. A thing finite is that which can be limited (terminari potest) by another thing of the same nature—ergo, body is said to be finite because it can always be conceived as larger. So thought is limited by other thoughts. But body does not limit thought, nor thought limit body.

III. By substance I understand that which is in itself, and is conceived per se—that is, the conception of which does not require the conception of anything else as antecedent to it.

IV. By attribute I understand that which the mind perceives as constituting the very essence of substance.

V. By modes I understand the accidents

(affectiones) of substance; or that which is in something else, through which also it is conceived.

VI. By God I understand the being absolutely infinite; that is, the substance consisting of infinite attributes, each of which expresses an infinite and eternal essence.

Explication, I say absolutely infinite, but not in suo genere; for to whatever is infinite, but not in suo genere, we can deny infinite attributes; but that which is absolutely infinite, to its essence pertains everything which implies essence, and involves no negation.

VII. That thing is said to be free which exists by the sole necessity of its nature, and by itself alone is determined to action. But that is necessary, or rather constrained, which owes its existence to another, and acts according to certain and determinate causes.

VIII. By eternity I understand existence itself, in as far as it is conceived necessarily to follow from the sole definition of an eternal thing.

It will be necessary for the reader to remember that Spinoza commenced his philosophical studies at the same point with Descartes. Both recognized existence as the primal fact, self-evident and indisputable. But while Descartes had, in some manner, fashioned a quality—God and God-created substance—Spinoza only found one, substance, the definition of which included existence.

Much has been said of Spinoza's "God" and "Divine Substance," and we must refer the reader to Definition Six, in which God is defined as being "infinite substance." Now, although we should be content to strike the word "God" out of our own tablet of philosophical nomenclature, as being a much misused, misrepresented, and entirely useless word, yet we must be very careful, when we find another man using the word, to get his precise definition, and not to use any-other ourselves while in his company.

Spinoza, when asked "What name do you attach to infinite substance?" says, "God."—If he had said any other word we could not have quarreled with him so long as he defined the word. Which he does here in the following way.

> *I can only take cognizance of one substance (of which I am part) having infinite attributes of extension and thought. I take cognizance of substance by its modes, and in my consciousness of existence. Everything is a mode of the attribute of extension, every thought, wish, or feeling, a mode of the attribute of thought. I call this, substance, with infinite attributes, God.*

Spinoza, like all other thinkers, found himself overpowered by the illimitable vastness of the infinite when attempting to grasp it by his own mental powers, but unlike other men he did not endeavor to relieve himself by separating himself from that infinite but by acknowledging he was a part of the whole.

The great translator of his works William Maccall says of Spinoza, "In the glorious throng of heroic names, there are few nobler than Spinoza's. Apart altogether from the estimate we may form of his philosophy, there is something unspeakably interesting in the life and the character of the man. In his metaphysical system there are two things exceedingly distinct. There is, first, the immense and prodigious, but terrible mathematical skeleton, which his subtle intellect binds up and throws as calmly into space as we drop a pebble into the water, and whose bones, striking against the wreck of all that is sacred in belief, or bold in speculation, rattle a wild response to our wildest phantasies, and drive us almost to think in despair that thinking is madness; and there is, secondly, the divinest vision of the infinite, and the divinest incense which the intuition of the infinite ever yet poured forth at the altar of creation."

The "Treatise on Politics" is not Spinoza's greatest work but there are still in politics certain eternal principles. In the second chapter of that Treatise, after defining what he means by nature, he proceeds as follows:

But many believe that the ignorant disturb more than follow the order of nature, and conceive of men in nature as a state within the state. For they assert that the human mind has not been produced by any natural causes, but created immediately by God, and thereby rendered so independent of other things as to have absolute power of determining itself, and of using reason aright. But experience teaches us more than enough, that it is no more in our power to have a sound mind than a sound body. Since everything, as far as it is able, strives to conserve its being, we cannot doubt that if it were equally in our power to live according to the prescripts of reason, as to be led by blind desire, all would seek the guidance of reason and live wisely, which is not the case. For every one is the slave of the particular pleasure to which he is most attached. Nor do theologians remove the difficulty when they assert that this inability is a vice, or a sin of human nature, which derives its origin from the fall of the first parent. For if it was in the power of the first man to stand rather than to fall, and if he was sound in faculty, and had perfect control over his own mind, how did it happen that he, the wise and prudent, fell? How could it happen that the first man in possession of his mental faculties, and master of his will, should be both open to temptation, and suffer himself to be robbed of his mind? For if he had the power of using his reason aright, he could not be deceived.

Spinoza here lays challenge to the notion that a human being with a sound ability to reason would ever consent to the Fall. And that it, therefore, must have been that Adam was a man of passion as much as he was a man of reason.

One can perhaps see here both an argument about human nature and an attempt by Spinoza to make sense of his own experience with the church. For was it not in both the cases of Adam and Baruch that curiosity about greater knowledge, rather than passion, led to exile?

Lewes, in his seventh chapter on Modern Philosophy, thus sums up Spinoza's teachings and their result. He states:

"The doctrine of Spinoza was of great importance, if for nothing more than having brought about the first crisis in modern philosophy. His doctrine was so clearly stated, and so rigorously deduced from admitted premises, that he brought philosophy into the following dilemma:

'Either my premises are correct; and we must admit that every clear and distinct idea is absolutely true; true not only subjectively, but objectively. If so, my objection is true; Or my premises are false; the voice of consciousness is not the voice of truth;

And if so, then is my system false, but all philosophy is impossible; since the only ground of certitude—our consciousness—is pronounced unstable, our only means of knowing the truth is pronounced fallacious.'

Spinozism or skepticism, choose between them, for you have no other choice."

Mankind refused, however, to make a choice. If the principles which Descartes had established could have no other result than Spinozism, it was worthwhile inquiring whether those principles might not themselves be modified.

The ground of discussion was shifted, psychology took the place of ontology. It was Descartes's theory of knowledge which led to

Spinozism; that theory must therefore he examined; that theory becomes the great subject of discussion. Before deciding upon the merits of any system which embraced the great questions of creation, the Deity, immortality, etc., men saw that it was necessary to decide upon the competency of the human mind to solve such problems. All knowledge must be obtained either through experience or independent of experience. Knowledge dependent on experience must necessarily be merely knowledge of phenomena. All are agreed that experience can only be experience of ourselves as modified by objects. All are agreed that to know things per se—noumena—we must know them through some other channel then experience. Have we or have we not that other channel? Can we transcend the sphere of our consciousness, and know things per se?

Spinoza's answer involves positing three different kinds of knowledge. The first kind being that of mutilated or confused random experience or imagination. The second being from our common knowledge and adequate ideas about the properties of things. And the third being from what Spinoza called "intuitive knowledge." Spinoza describes intuitive knowledge in the following way.

> *This kind of knowing proceeds from an adequate idea of certain attributes of God to the adequate knowledge of the essence of things.*

Thus Spinoza, who as a young man had been forced out of the synagogue, became a favorite of many clergymen. For what he was ultimately saying was that God could not only be seen in reality but actually was in a way the only thing which allowed us to see the reality of things! Spinoza, in his Ethics, famously puts it in the following way:

> *Whatsoever is, is in God, and without God nothing can be, or be conceived.*

And this "intuitive knowledge" means that in very practical ways human beings can now trust their intuitions. And in teaching us to trust our intuitions Spinoza, despite any of his faults, has now become a key figure in the history of freethinking!

EDITH STEIN

Edith Stein was born on October 12, 1891 in Breslau, Germany. She says of her birth:

> *I was born on the Day of Atonement and my mother always considered it my real birthday.*

For a Jew the Day of Atonement is the holiest day of the year. It commemorates the day the high priest would enter the Holy of Holies, a special chamber in the Old Testament Jerusalem temple, in order to offer a yearly sacrifice for the expiation of the sins of the people. Being a devout Jew Edith's mother Auguste was well aware of the great symbolism of the day of her seventh child's birth. Edith says of it:

> *She laid great stress on my being born on the Day of Atonement, and I believe this contributed more than anything else to her youngest being especially dear to her.*

Another event of Edith's early life reinforced this notion of her mother Auguste that she was a special child. Edith's father, Siegfried, ran a lumber company and when Edith was two years old he was about to leave on a business trip in order to survey a forest. After all the farewells had been said and he had started on his way Edith suddenly called him back for one last hug and goodbye. While on this survey he died suddenly from a seizure leaving Edith's mother a young widow with seven children to care for.

Auguste was up to the task and set about making the lumber company a success. This led to her spending long hours away from home causing Edith to be raised mostly by her older sister Else. Edith was a bright, rambunctious and strong willed child. Her older sister Else was studying to be a teacher and would try out various child training methods on Edith with little success. Yet finally, at age seven, Edith made the conscious choice to trust the judgment of her older sister, and mother, and thus became a much more manageable child.

This power to contemplate the wisdom of her older sister, and mother, and accept it at such a young age shows evidence of Edith's great gifts for reason and inner contemplation even as a child. She says of them:

> *Within me, however, there was a hidden world. Whatever I saw or heard throughout my days was pondered there.*

Perhaps due to these abilities Edith became a very bright student and even began to show signs of being a gifted teacher. She started giving a sort of "pre-lecture" to the other students in her school geography class (taught at the time by the school principal). She says of it:

> *Eventually the principal caught on it seems but apparently had no objections; in any case, once when one of the others gave an incorrect answer, he calmly inquired of me whether I had failed to coach them correctly.*

Edith's powers of inner contemplation were to have other effects on her childhood. For from about age 13 she began to become preoccupied by many deep, almost philosophical, questions. She speaks of them as having been "ideological" in nature. In any case they were definitely not a part of the normal school curriculum for a 13 year old. For this reason she began to lose interest in her studies and finally asked her mother if she could leave school altogether. Steadfast in her belief that Edith was a special child Auguste allowed her to do so.

Yet the inner crisis had effects beyond just this. For it was at about this same point in time that Edith "deliberately and consciously" made the choice not to pray any longer. This despite the fact that her mother was a devout Jew. Since Edith abandoned this basic act of prayer at such an early age she should never be thought of here as having had a mature Jewish faith. It was rather the faith of a child which simply failed to come to maturity.

Edith's older sister Else had married a physician and moved to Hamburg. It was decided that Edith should be sent there to help out the young couple with household chores and to serve as a sort of moral support for her sister. The marriage was not going well and Else confided in Edith all the details, perhaps more than a child her age should have heard, which may have given her a rather negative view of married life in general. Finally, it all got to be too much for Edith and she returned home to Breslau.

Upon her return she had a great deal of free time and began to read voraciously. She read Grillparzer, Hebbel, Ibsen, and, especially, Shakespeare. Yet her first venture into philosophical reading met with some resistance:

> The day I produced Schopenhauer's _The World as Will and Idea_ my older sisters protested energetically. They feared for my

*mental health; and I had to return the two
volumes to the library unread.*

One wonders what might have become of
Edith as a philosopher had her sisters had
their way.

Edith greatly enjoyed this time in her life
yet realized that she would have to make a
decision about the next direction to go in
soon. Her family offered many gentle hints,
which she listened to politely, yet she had her
own method of discerning her path:

> *I could not act unless I had an inner
> compulsion to do so. My decisions arose out of
> a depth that was unknown even to myself.*

This almost otherworldly source of decision
making gave Edith a great sense of certitude
about her ability to bring her decisions about.
Once she had this certitude about a particular
decision she let no obstacle get in her path.
She says of it:

I found it an intriguing kind of sport to overcome hindrances which were apparently insurmountable.

The decision was made for Edith to take the examination for the Obersekunda, a level of school normally reached at age 16, and thus bypass three years of normal instruction. Private tutors were called in and some family members also served in the role. Edith's cousin Richard Courant organized the effort and also served as the math tutor. Some of the other subjects were Latin, French, English and History. When her Cousin Richard's career took him to Göttingen, where the two would later cross paths, Edith took charge of hiring the tutors herself.

Despite all of this work, which only allowed her to see her family at meals, Edith enjoyed this time in her life. She speaks of it as the first time her mental powers were fully engaged in a task for which they were well suited. Edith was the only student at her exam accepted to the Obersekunda.

After joining the Obersekunda Edith became one of the best students in her class. She especially excelled in her study of Latin. During the time of her tutoring, she had discovered the beauty and precision of Latin. Her exceptional abilities in it would one day allow her to translate such spiritual luminaries as Thomas Aquinas and John Henry Newman into German for the first time.

As Edith's studies at the Obersekunda drew to a close the pressure to choose a career path grew. Many of her family members had chosen such practical fields as law and medicine so when Edith stated her wish to study literature and philosophy, at a family gathering no less, it was not met with universal approval. For the only career path such a study might lead to was one of teaching at a Gymnasium. For even the thought of a woman rising any further in the teaching profession was out of the question in the Germany of those days. Yet one must always keep in mind Edith's sport of overcoming insurmountable obstacles.

In 1911 Edith began her studies at the University of Breslau. Despite her intention to study literature and philosophy it was the study of psychology which would dominant the four semesters she was to spend there. This was because of the fine professor of psychology William Stern. It was while taking one of his courses that Edith was first exposed to the thought of Edmund Husserl. While she was studying various essays on the psychology of thought her friend George Moskiewicz approached her and said:

> *"Leave all that stuff aside," he said, "and just read this; after all, it is where all the others got their ideas." He handed me a thick book: the second Volume of Husserl's Logische Untersuchungen. I would have pounced on it at once but could not; my semester assignments would not permit it. Yet I determined to devote my next vacation to it.*

After this she saw an illustrated journal with a picture of one of Husserl's highly talented female students, Hegwig Marthesis, on the cover of it. Next, she heard that her cousin Richard Courant had obtained a position at the same university as Husserl. Add to this the many idyllic tales circulating at the time about philosophizing in the streets of Göttingen and Edith's mind was made up. She would spend the summer semester of 1913 studying under Edmund Husserl.

When Edith arrived in Göttingen in late April of 1913 only 15 months remained until the beginning of World War I. The war would change her world forever and effectively end the Göttingen School of Phenomenology. Many of its German members would choose military service. Some of the foreigners who had come to study would get caught up in the nationalistic fervor of the day and end up in internment camps. Edith herself would choose to become a nurse at a military hospital. Yet she would have three semesters of student life in Göttingen before all of this took place and she intended to put them to very good use.

In those days a student could not attend a professor's lectures until they had been accepted by said professor through a personal interview. Such was the purpose of Edith Stein's first meeting with Edmund Husserl. Although Husserl had heard favorable things about Stein already, of help in this interview was the fact that Edith had arrived in Göttingen having read both of Husserl's major works on phenomenology.

> *When I mentioned my name, he said, "Dr. Reinach has spoken to me about you. How much of my work have you read?" "The Logische Untersuchungen." (The first volume of Logische Untersuchungen published in 1900, was epoch-making because in it Husserl radically criticized the then prevailing psychologism and all relativism. The second volume appeared in the following year. It far*

surpassed its predecessor in significance as well as in bulk. Here for the first time Husserl treated problems in logic with the method which he later developed systematically into the "phenomenological method" and which expanded to cover the entire area of philosophy.) "All of the Logische Untersuchungen? He asked me. "Volume Two--all of it." "All of Volume Two? Why, that's a heroic achievement!" he said, smiling. With that, I was accepted.

Since the time of Kant philosophy had been in a position where it could not posit any direct connection between the human mind and objects in the actual world. Kant had seen the human mind as being a sort of a filter of direct experience. Later thinkers had developed his ideas into "psychologism" which was a popular, yet much criticized, form of thought at that time. What was novel about phenomenology is that it was making the claim that the human mind could be connected to objects in the actual world

through the "phenomenological method."
This was the "new world" that Edith Stein
had now stepped into.

At the end of the summer Edith decided
to study under Husserl permanently and thus
went to him in order to request a doctoral
theme. Edith had been taking Husserl's
course on "Nature and Spirit" that first
semester. In it he had said that an objective
outer world could only be known through a
plurality of individuals relating to one another
intersubjectively. He had used the term
"Einfhlung" (Empathy) to describe this
intersubjectivity yet in no place had he
detailed the nature of it. As Edith put it,
"Here was a lacuna to be filled." Husserl
agreed and Edith had her doctoral theme.

Having been introduced to Stein as a
person and seen her intellectual formation let
us now examine her understanding of
empathy. She begins by pointing out the
distinction between the physical body and the
living body. The physical body is an object

we perceive, like many others, yet in a different and specific way. She states:

> *Every other object is given to me in an infinitely variable multiplicity of appearances and of changing positions, and there are also times when it is not given to me. But this one object (my physical body) is given to me in successive appearances only variable within very narrow limits. As long as I have my eyes open at all, it is continually there with steadfast obtrusiveness, always having the same tangible nearness as no other object has. It is always "here" while other objects are always "there."*

It would seem that Stein is referring here only to the sensory data of the physical body. For whenever I open my eyes or engage in self-touch my physical body remains present through this sensory data. Yet what if I close my eyes and stretch out my limbs inside of a decompression chamber? Even in this state, where I have no sensory data of my physical body at all, my sense of embodiment remains inescapably present. The fact that I know this body belongs to me can never be known by outer perception alone because outer perception would involve only interrupted streams of sensory data while my sense of embodiment remains constant. This constant sense of embodiment, given to me only outside of sensory data, is my "living body."

The living body is not given to me as a sensation, or as a group of sensations, but rather as the focal point of all of my sensations. It thus has an entirely different nature than that of my physical body.

> *All these entities from which my sensations arise are amalgamated into a unity, the unity of my living body, and they are themselves places in the living body.*

Through this Edith Stein begins to speak of the living body as having a "zero point of orientation" which she refers to as the "I." She presents the example of a foreign physical object which could approach my living body, and even appear to be closer to my "I" than one of the outer limbs of my living body (or the sense of embodiment of said outer limb). Is this foreign physical object now closer to my zero point of orientation than my own outer limb? Edith Stein answers:

> *The distance of the parts of my*
> *living body from me is completely*
> *incomparable with the distance of*
> *foreign physical bodies from me.*
> *The living body as a whole is at the*
> *zero point of orientation with all*
> *physical bodies outside of it.*
> *"Body space" [Leibraum] and*
> *"outer space" are completely*
> *different from each other.*

The problem remaining here for Stein is that one's own physical body can be perceived with the senses just as foreign physical objects are. Therefore, from the standpoint of the senses, what separates the two?

Stein has been speaking strictly of a body at rest up until this point. Yet once a body is put into motion a further understanding of the relationship between the living body and the physical body becomes possible.

> *When I move one of my limbs,*

besides becoming bodily aware of
my own movement, I have an outer
visual or tactile perception of
physical body movements to which
the limb's changed appearances
testify. As the bodily perceived and
outwardly perceived limb are
interpreted as the same, so there
also arises an identical coincidence
of the living and physical body's
movement.

This constant sense of fusion between the living body and the physical body is one that cannot be broken. For wherever my physical body goes my living body must follow in an almost perfect and "indissoluble" union.

In terms of the phenomenological reduction Edith Stein points out that no matter what standpoint one takes in order to gain a perspective on a given object the physical body and the living body remain in this always and indissoluble union:

Every step I take discloses a new bit
of the world to me or I see the old

one from a new side. In doing so I
always take my living body along.
Not only am I always "here" but
also it is; the various "distance" of
its parts from me are only variations
within this "here."

Thus, the living body and the physical body are both necessary in order to perform the phenomenological reduction.

Stein now seeks to delve more deeply into the relationship between the living body and the physical body through the foot "gone to sleep" example. She describes the foot "gone to sleep" as being beyond the realm of the living body because of its lack of sensation. Like a "foreign physical body that I cannot shake off." Yet when circulation returns and the foot awakes it once again becomes a part of the living body. Stein points out the implications of this.

For the living body is essentially
constituted through sensations;
sensations are the real constituents
of consciousness and, as such,

belong to the "I." Thus how could
there be a living body not the body
of an "I"!

Thus the concepts of the living body, the physical body and the "I" are joined together.

Stein now goes on to investigate the relationship between the living body and feelings. She points out that this relationship is somewhat similar to the phenomenon of fusion already discussed between the living body and the physical body. However, one could wish to express a cheerful feeling yet be simply too physically tired to do so. She refers to this as "the phenomenon of the reciprocal action of psychic and somatic experiences." By this she means that the psychic depends upon the somatic in order to understand experiences. The consciousness of the "I" is always body bound.

Feelings have another characteristic for Stein. They are never complete in themselves but always seek bodily expression.

Feeling in its pure essence is not

> *something complete in itself. As it*
> *were, it is loaded with an energy*
> *which must be unloaded.*

She goes on to point out some of the many different ways a person might express feelings with bodily expression being the most normative among them. And although the bodily expression of feeling can be faked, expressed only in terms of the physical body, the actual phenomenon of the expression of feeling is a rather definite process.

> *I not only feel how feeling is*
> *poured into expression and*
> *"unloaded" in it, but at the same*
> *time I have this expression given in*
> *bodily perception. The smile in*
> *which my pleasure is experientially*
> *externalized is at the same time*
> *given to me as a stretching of my*
> *lips.*

So while it is possible to simply stretch your lips without the accompanying feeling and sense of unloading of said feeling in expression, the actual phenomenon of the expression of a feeling is a much more complex and definite experience.

This leads Edith Stein into a discussion of the role of the will within the psycho-physical individual. She sees the will not just as a mechanism of choice isolated in itself but as always seeking to be connected to action in a similar way as feelings always seek to be connected to expression.

> *The will employs a psycho-physical mechanism to fulfill itself, to realize what is willed, just as feeling uses such a mechanism to realize its expression.*

With the main difference here being that the existence of feelings is something a person has little control over while the will by its nature is a voluntarily controlled function.

However, this begs an important question which should not be passed over. Edith Stein now moves on to the question of whether the will is causally determined. If the choices we make now are really our own or just the result of a long line of causality which we no longer have any control over?

> *Action is always the creation of what is not. This process can be carried out in causal succession, but the initiation of the process, the true intervention of the will is not experienced as a causal but as a special effect.*

Stein holds that causality plays a role in the will but only in terms of it being a conditioning factor. Such as when I will my body to move when it is very tired. Yet she maintains: *"All these causal relationships are external to the essence of the will."*

Stein now sums up what we have learned so far about the psycho-physical individual.

> *The psycho-physical individual as a whole belongs to the order of nature. The living body in contrast with the physical body is characterized by having fields of sensation, being located at the zero point of orientation of the spatial world, moving voluntarily and*

being constructed of moving organs, being the field of expression of the experiences of its "I" and the instrument of the "I's" will.

Given this information, the next natural question arises. How empathy toward the foreign individual possible?

Edith Stein starts with the example of the inner perception of the living body being "co-given" with the outer perception of the physical body within a given individual. This fusion between the living body and the physical body of the individual then allows him or her to observe the foreign individual's living body and physical body being given in this same way. Once this is understood one can transpose their living body onto the foreign physical body of the other and begin to form an "empathic representation" of it.

Thus, the key to understanding empathy is contained within the individual. For once I understand the relationship between my living body and my physical body all I need to do to is act as if the foreign physical body is my own physical body through putting my living body into relationship with it (either through fantasy or representations of my own past experience). She speaks of seeing someone's hand pressing on a table. If I wish to understand the sensations of this hand I simply act as if the foreign physical hand is my own physical hand and, by either recalling a time my hand was pressing on a table or by engaging in a fantasy about a possible experience, enter into relationship with it. Edith Stein refers to this act as a "co-comprehension" between my living body and the foreign physical hand.

Edith Stein more explicitly defines this new term while summing up the nature of sensual empathy. Notice the key role that the relationship between the living body and the physical body plays:

> *The possibility of sensual empathy is warranted by the interpretation of our own living body as a physical body and our own physical body as a living body because of the fusion of outer and bodily perception. It is also warranted by the possibility of spatially altering this physical body, and finally by the*

possibility of modifying its real properties in fantasy while retaining its type.

Thus, it is through a proper understanding of the nature of our own body and sense of embodiment that empathy for the foreign individual may become possible.

Stein's insights into the nature of empathy serve as a foundation for that one thing that is at the heart of all good communities, societies, and ethics—empathy. For this alone she is worthy to be put among our collection of history's great freethinkers. Yet for Stein this was only the beginning. For these same principles of empathy led directly to her theory of feminism. And her feminism led to The Theology of the Body of Pope John Paul II. And this is not to even begin to mention her many later works or the great witness of her life and martyrdom. For all of these reasons Edith Stein is not just a great freethinker, but perhaps the greatest woman of our time! [1]

---

[1] Parts of this section are taken from the Chaos To Order Publishing book The Transposition of Edith Stein: Her Contributions to

Philosophy, Feminism, and The Theology of the Body.